J
306.8   Fitz-Gerald,   c.1
FI   Christine

I can be a mother

$12.60

DATE		
FE 21 '91	NOV 29 94	NOV 27 98
MY 13 '91	OCT 11 95	MY 18 '99
JY 27 '91	FEB 20 '96	AG 13 '01
AG 13 '91	AUG 26 96	AG 27 02
AG 23 '91	SP 18 98	JA 30 03
SE 25 '91	NOV 04 96	JE 21 '04
MR 18 '92	APR 02 97	JE 15 09
SE 14 '92	OCT 23 97	FE 06 16
MY 26 '93	NOV 03 97	N 05 17
DEC 18 '93	FEB 10 98	JE 05 18
JUL 28 '94	APR 16 98	

© THE BAKER & TAYLOR CO.

I CAN BE A

MOTHER

By Christine Fitz-Gerald

Prepared under the direction of Robert Hillerich, Ph.D.

 CHILDRENS PRESS ®

CHICAGO

Library of Congress Cataloging-in-Publication Data

Fitz-Gerald, Christine Maloney.
  I can be a mother.

  Includes index.
  Summary: Describes the qualities, roles, activities,
and occupations of mothers and explores the differences
between human and animal mothers.
  1.   Mothers—United States—Juvenile literature.
2.   Mother and child—United States—Juvenile literature.
[1.   Mothers. 2.   Mother and child.] I.   Title.
HQ759.F58   1988   306.8'743   87-35189
  ISBN O-516-O1914-7

Childrens Press®, Chicago
Copyright ©1989 by Regensteiner Publishing Enterprises, Inc.
All rights reserved. Published simultaneously in Canada.
Printed in the United States of America.
1 2 3 4 5 6 7 8 9 1O R 98 97 96 95 94 93 92 91 9O 89

PICTURE DICTIONARY

learning

instincts

skills

reason　　**solve problems**

teaching

parents

adopt

talent

stepmother

Human babies need their mothers.
They cannot take care of themselves.

Raising a child from a newborn baby to an adult is a big job. Newborn babies are helpless. They need a mother to feed, bathe, dress, carry and cuddle them, and keep them from harm.

No animal baby grows as slowly or needs its mother for as long a time as a human baby does. A baby zebra can run with the herd when it is only one hour old. An hour-old-human baby

Polar bear (left) and wolf cubs (right)

can't hold up his or her
head alone. A one-year-old
polar bear weighs 200
pounds and lives and hunts
alone. A one-year-old baby
is just learning to walk and to
use a spoon. Wolf cubs and
sperm whales are among

A killer whale calf can swim as soon as it is born.

the few animals that live
with their mothers for two
or three years. Children
usually live with their
parents until they are
eighteen years old or older.

Baby geese (left) and baby deer (right)

instincts

Why do human beings grow up so much more slowly than animals? Animals have a head start because they are born with instincts. From the moment they are born, instincts tell animals what to do. A baby deer knows it must hide

8

Baby turtles race to the ocean.

and stay very still while its mother is gone. Baby sea turtles know they must race down the beach for the ocean. No one taught the deer or the turtles what to do. They were born knowing. They were born with these instincts.

Human children must be taught to brush their teeth (left) and to walk (right).

learning

skills

Human children are not like animals. They are not born knowing the skills that they need to live. They must learn these skills. This learning takes years.

Children learn from their
teachers at school (top),
from their friends (bottom left),
and from their mothers (bottom right).

Humans can learn to use a computer to help them solve problems.

reason   solve problems

However, after what seems like a slow start, human beings have one huge advantage over animals. Humans can reason and solve problems. They can think. Therefore, they can learn far more than animals.

Some mothers are good at sports. They can teach
their children how to ski (left) or swim (right).

Parents are a child's most
important teachers.
Mothers want their children
to learn to live without
them. This is a big job and
there is no one right way to
do it. Mothers are alike in
only one way; they are all
women. But each mother

teaching

parents

Cooking is fun when mother and daughter work together.

talent

will have her own way of child raising because each mother is an individual.

Mothers have different talents. Some are good at sports. Some are good cooks. One may be able to fix cars. Another may be able to sew clothes.

Mothers use different talents to show their children how to ride a bike (top left), color Easter eggs (top right), or plant flowers (bottom).

Some mothers work at
home and run the house.
Others work outside the
home and run the house.
Some mothers are judges,
waitresses, doctors,
teachers, interior
decorators, police officers,
or sales people.

Some mothers work outside
the home as carpenters (top),
waitresses (bottom left),
or dentists (bottom right).

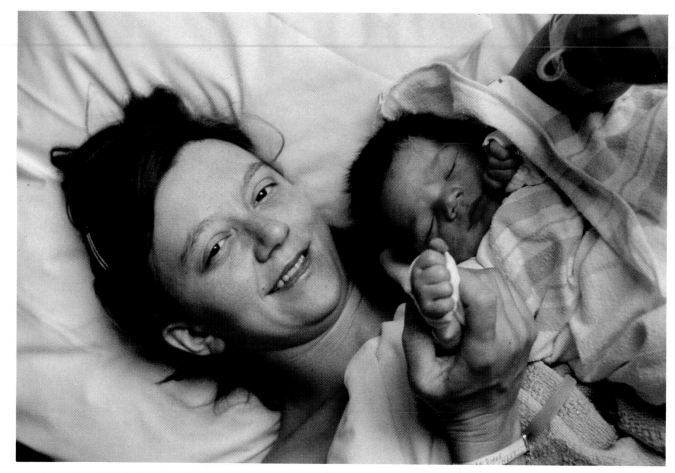
A mother holds her new baby.

adopt

Most mothers give birth to their children. Some mothers adopt. They take another woman's child to love and raise as their own.

Stepmothers are mothers
by marriage. They care for
their husband's children.

stepmother

Stepmothers show they care in
the things they do everyday.

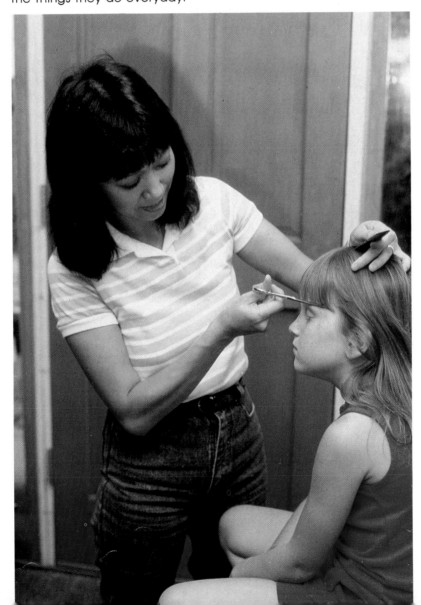

19

Families enjoy playing games together.

In many families both the mother and father share in raising the children. In some families, however, only the mother lives with her children. She has a hard job.

A mother and child share a special bond

What makes a mother? It's not whether she is the birth mother or the stepmother. Nor is it how much time she spends at home each day. It doesn't matter how well she cooks or keeps the house. What

All children need good food (left) and proper clothing (right).

sets a mother apart is the love that she has for her children and the fact that she has taken on the job of caring for them.

All children need love. Children of all ages also need good food, clothing,

22

Babies need special care and attention.

and a safe home. A mother
gives different kinds of
attention to her children as
they grow.

Babies need their
mothers all the time.
Older children need their
mothers, too.

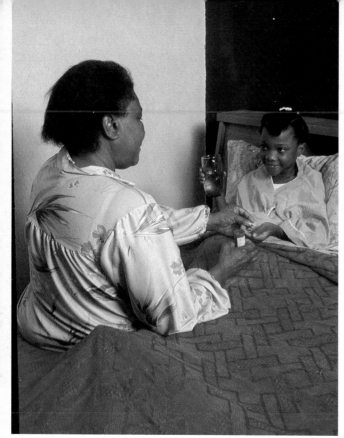

Mothers care for children when they are sick (left) or hurt (right).

All children need someone to help them. They need someone to care for them when they are sick and cheer them when they are hurt or disappointed.

Spinning wool (left) or shopping wisely (right) are
two skills mothers can teach older children.

Older children do many
things for themselves, but
they still need a mother to
listen to them, encourage
them, teach them skills
such as handling money,
and help them with their
problems.

25

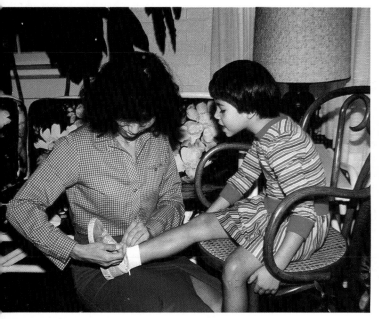

Children learn to tie shoes (left) and grow
plants (right) by watching their mothers.

Mothers do all of this and
more. Some things, such as
tying shoes, they set out to
teach. But mothers also
teach things without trying,
just by giving an example.

Children see their mothers
solving everyday problems
and dealing with other
people. They learn their
mother's ideas about what
is important, what is right
and wrong.

Humans need to receive and give love to others.

Animal mothers part from their young and never see them again. Or, if they do meet, they do not know their own children. Human mothers and children are bonded together by deep, lifelong love.

Being a mother is not easy, but mothers say that

it is the best thing that they
have ever done. The love
between mother and child
makes the years of work
worthwhile. Mothers have
the joy of seeing their
children change and grow.

WORDS YOU SHOULD KNOW

adopt(uh • DAHPT) — bring into a family through legal steps someone else's child and raise as one's own

adult(uh • DUHLT) — a person who has reached legal age of 18

advantage(ad • VAN • tij) — something more likely to be successful; benefit

bonded(BOND • id) — held firmly together

cuddle(KUD • il) — to hold closely, hug

disappointed(diss • ah • POYN • tid) — unhappy that one's hopes failed

encourage(en • KER • ij) — to help, to give hope

handling(HAN • dling) — managing, controlling, taking care of

human(HYOO • min) — a person; man, woman, or child

ideas(eye • DEE • uz) — thoughts, understandings

individual(in • dih • VID • joo • il) — one person

instincts(IN • stinkts) — feelings or actions one knows naturally, without instruction

learning(LER • ning) — beginning to understand through instruction and experience

parents(PAIR • intz) — a person's father and mother

reason(REE • zun) —to think through a problem using known facts

safe(SAIF) —having no danger or evil

skills(SKILZ) —expertness one develops through training and practice

stepmother(STEP • muh • ther) —a father's wife, who is not the mother of his children

talent(TAL • ent) —a natural or acquired ability

worthwhile(werth • WYLE) —as valuable as the time or effort involved

INDEX

ABOUT THE AUTHOR

Christine Fitz-Gerald has a B.A. in English Literature from Ohio University and a Masters in Management from Northwestern University. She has been employed by the Quaker Oats Co. and by General Mills. Most recently, she was a strategic planner for a division of Honeywell, Inc. in Minneapolis. She now resides in Chicago with her husband and two young children.